If You Give a Girl a Giant

Study Guide

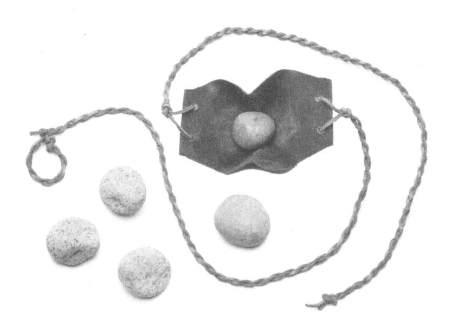

If You Give A Girl A Giant...

Study Guide

Six-Week Study

Karen Porter

Bold Vision Books
PO Box 2011
Friendswood, Texas 77549

Copyright @ Karen Porter 2019

ISBN 978-1946708-335

Published in the United States of America.
Published by Bold Vision Books, PO Box 2011, Friendswood,
Texas 77549

Cover Art by © James Steidl
Cover Design by Maddie Scott

Table of Contents

Introduction

Welcome to study of *If You Give a Girl a Giant*. Thank you for reading the book and for taking a closer look into this fascinating passage of Scripture. If you are studying with a group, please let me know by sending an email to kaeporter@gmail.com. I would love to connect with your group while you are reading and studying the book together. If you are going through this study guide alone, I invite you to connect with me at kaeporter@gmail.com. I would love to hear your thoughts.

Giants are real. We face them each day even though we may not recognize the magnitude of their influence. Your battle is genuine. When you battle with a giant, you need tools. But the tools the world suggests, such as *pull yourself up by your boot straps* or *take control of your life,* don't always help us win the battle. We need supernatural help. And in this short Bible passage, hidden within the meanings of the names of giants and warriors, we find His weapons—which never fail.

I have been forever changed by the message of the giants and the warriors who defeated them. I pray you will be encouraged, emboldened, and challenged to fight for your life.

Karen Porter

Every **person** who
never **killed** a **giant**
will **tell you**
it's impossible

About this Study

Thank you for choosing to read *If You Give a Girl a Giant* and for embarking on this six-week study of the book. I am praying you will find the tools you need to Fight For Your Life. Because you are worth it…God says so in Ephesians 2:10:

"For we are God's masterpiece…"

How to Use This Study Guide

Each week is divided into 6 days and each week has a memory verse for you to memorize. On the days when the guide asks you to read a chapter or numerous pages, there are only a few questions to answer in the study guide. Use these days to read thoroughly in the book and highlight or mark any sections that stand out to you or where you have a question. Some days, there are no pages to read in the book; instead we dig deeper into the methods of the giant or the power of the weapon. Use these days to fully understand how the enemy attacks you and how wonderfully God protects you with His weapons. On the sixth day of each week, the guide asks you to answer the questions in the related *What's a Girl to Do?* chapter and reflect about what you can do to be victorious.

Your giants may show up physically or mentally or spiritually or emotionally. But never doubt that these giants are real. They strut and shout and attack when you least expect them.

I am praying for you as you fight your giants and turn to the Lord for all your answers.

Karen

The giant of discouragement arrives when we least expect him.

#ifyougiveagirlagiant

Week 1 – The Giant of Discouragement

Memory Verse for the week:

Don't be afraid, for I am with you.
Don't be discouraged, for I am your God.
I will strengthen you and help you.
I will hold you up with my victorious right hand (Isaiah 41:10)

This week we will face the giant of discouragement. He looms large in your life and mine. He attacks when we are feeling great, and he attacks when we are feeling low. One hurtful word can take you down the slippery slope of gloom and pessimism. And if disappointments strike us over and over, we are in danger of falling into the mindset of despair and hopelessness. We try to fight the giant of discouragement with positive thinking or we try to make lifestyle changes or we set goals and plans, but we cannot face the giant alone.

Day One – Read: Prologue, Introduction, and Chapter 1, The Giant pages 13-34

What one idea stands out to you in the story of David and Goliath?

_____

_____

_____

_____

In the introduction (beginning on page 17), the author discusses the Goliath each person faces—his or her decision to follow Christ as personal savior. Have you received His gift of salvation? If so, write about it in the space below. If not, will you ask someone in your group to pray with you and for you?

_____

_____

_____

_____

The author discusses how giants lurk around us in daily life perhaps hovering over us as if in our backyard. What giants have you faced?

_____

_____

_____

_____

In the verses quoted on page 22 from 2 Samuel 21, David is described as old and tired. Yet the giants showed up again to torment him and his men. Why do you think our battles with giants seem never ending?

_____

_____

_____

_____

Day Two – Facing Discouragement

What do you think is the best definition for discouragement?

_____

_____

_____

_____

Discouragement often begins with disappointment. In each of the categories below, list your disappointments with:

People you meet:_____

Relatives and Friends: _____

Daily Living: _____

Yourself: _____

Acquaintances, co-workers, relatives and friends don't always under-stand you or your situation. When people refuse to take you seriously or understand, it frustrates you and brings discouragement.

Daily living is often routine and leads to exasperation with the repetition. Someone said, "Life is just so *daily*." Every mom knows that the routine of laundry and house cleaning feels never ending. American poet, Henry Van Dyke warned us about the dangers of daily boredom. He said, "As long as habit and routine dictate the pattern of living, new dimensions of the soul will not emerge."

It is also easy to get disappointed with God, especially when it seems we are in limbo. And the waiting cause us to lose hope.

Much of my discouragement is birthed in my inner spirit—my self—those *I did it again, moments.*

Life coach and author, Leslie Vernick, gives us a list of steps that can help us overcome discouragement. Listed below are the five actions she recommends. Beside each one, write how you think this tool might help you with discouragement.

Absolute Honesty: _____

_____

Healthy Eating and Exercise: _____

_____

Thought Life: _____

_____

Perspective: _____

_____

Closer to God: _____

_____

Discouragement is a common emotion that can lead to worse behaviors. When we are discouraged, we want comfort. Circle the comforts you seek when you feel discouraged.

Food	Shopping	Calling a Friend
Sleep	Isolation	Alcohol
Bite Your Nails	Denial	Sex

How does the Bible say we should react when discouraged? (Psalm 34:17-19).

_____

_____

_____

_____

What promise does God give us when we are discouraged? (Isaiah 41:10).

_____

_____

_____

_____

Read Matthew 11:2-6. Why do you think John the Baptist sent his men to ask Jesus if he [Jesus] was the Messiah?

_____

_____

_____

_____

Read 1 Kings 19:2-4. Why do you think Elijah was discouraged? (Hint: verse 2).

_____

_____

_____

_____

John the Baptist wondered if his life's work was a waste. He had been the forerunner for the Messiah, but now he was in jail, and it seemed as if Jesus was only a traveling preacher. John wanted to see the Kingdom of God, and now his sense of inactivity sent him down the discouragement trail. Elijah had two enormous ministry moments (1 Kings 18). First, he defeated 450 prophets of Baal on Mt Hermon, and then he successfully prayed down rain to end the drought. These successes were great, but the minute Jezebel threatened him, he raced away to a solitary place to mope.

Why do you think the enemy sends discouragement to us in the moments of our success?

_____

_____

_____

_____

Day Three – Read Chapter 2, pages 35-43 – The Weapon

God's weapon to destroy discouragement is His faithfulness. I was surprised because I've heard many other solutions. What other ways to fight discouragement have your heard about or read about?

_____

_____

_____

_____

How does knowing and believing that God is faithful help us fight discouragement?

_____

_____

_____

_____

Read 2 Corinthians 4:8-9. What does Paul's attitude about his troubles tell you about the faithfulness of God?

_____

_____

_____

_____

Read Philippians 4:19. What does God supply?

_____

_____

_____

_____

Read 1 Peter 1:6-8. How do these verses help you to rely on God's faithfulness?

_____

_____

_____

_____

Day Four – God's Faithfulness

Read Deuteronomy 7:9. How is God described and what will He do?

_____

_____

_____

_____

When I am discouraged, I go to a dark place in my spirit. It feels like a hole with no bottom. I can't seem to get a foothold or a grip to push myself out of the hole. I feel alone and abandoned. When I read Joshua 1:9, it dawned on me that I am never alone—even in my discouragement. What does that verse say about God?

_____

_____

_____

_____

Is God faithful even when I am not faithful? Explain. 2 Timothy 2:13.

_____

_____

_____

_____

Match the phrase with the Bible verse:

Psalm 34:17-19   Psalm 147:3   Psalm 55:22
Isaiah 41:10   Isaiah 40:31   Isaiah 42:6
Jeremiah 29:11

We shall soar like Eagles _____

God has plans for us _____

The Lord is near to the brokenhearted _____

He will sustain us _____

He is our God _____

God heals the broken and binds wounds _____

God guides us to level ground _____

Day Five – Read Chapter 3, pages 43-49 – Fighting for Your Life

On page 43, Karen quotes her pastor in the following statement. Fill in the blanks.

God is not the god of the _____;

He is the God of _____.

What did you learn about the difference between tweak and transformation?

_____

_____

_____

_____

Read 2 Peter 1:8 and Romans 8:29. What are God's plans for you?

_____

_____

_____

_____

Have you settled for a tweak?

In your health? _____

_____

In your finances? _____

_____

In your service for God? _____

_____

In your relationships? _____

_____

Write a prayer asking God to transform you instead of the tweak you've accepted?

_____

_____

_____

_____

The Journey from tweak to transformation requires a slow process of putting one foot after another. What step will you take this week toward transformation?

_____

_____

_____

_____

Day Six – Read Chapter 4, pages 51-62 – What's a Girl to Do?

As part of this day of reflection, answer the questions in the book on pages 52, 53, 54, 56, 58, 60, and 61. Be ready to discuss your answers with your group.

Week 2 – The Giant of Defeat
Memory Verse of the Week:

He reached down from on high and took hold of me;
he drew me out of deep waters.
He rescued me from my powerful enemy,
from my foes, who were too strong for me.
They confronted me in the day of my disaster,
but the LORD was my support (Psalm 18:16-18).

This week we face the giant of defeat. When our discouragement and disappointment and circumstances collide, we may experience the terrible sensation of having no hope. *No hope* feels as if every door has closed and the darkness is closing in. The weight of our past destroys the possibilities of the future. Many words—such as overwhelmed, despair, beaten, crushed, exhausted—describe the feelings, yet no word can fully define the knock-out of defeat.

Day One – Read Chapter 5, pages 65-72 – The Giant

What do you think is the difference between discouragement and defeat?

_____

_____

_____

_____

Describe a time when you felt the giant of defeat moving in.

_____

_____

_____

_____

What advice did friends of professionals give you when you felt defeated?

_____

_____

_____

_____

Why was that advice not enough to pull you from the grips of the giant?

_____

_____

_____

_____

Which of the story examples in this chapter touched you and gave you hope?

_____

_____

_____

_____

Day Two – Facing Defeat

Defeat is losing the battle. Defeat feels as if there is no hope and that God has abandoned you.

The giant of defeat attacks us when we allow situations to overwhelm our life and block out the light of the Lord. In the list below, circle any area where you feel you have lost the battle.

Illnesses or Injuries you've faced	Bad habits
Physical Pain	Chronic Pain
Personal weakness	Inability to confront
Too willing to confront	Weight issues
Friends who have disappointed you	Professional setbacks
Family who doesn't understand	Thought Patterns
Unhealthy choices you've made	Weight issues
Financial setbacks	Addiction
Failure in business	Failure with family

Other _____

Have you ever felt broken? Did you feel that God had abandoned you? Explain.

_____

_____

_____

_____

Is there an area of your life where you feel you have coped and coped but you can't cope anymore?

_____

_____

_____

_____

With God, no defeat is final. How does Luke 1:37 confirm this statement?

_____

_____

_____

_____

Day Three – Read Chapter 6, pages 73-83 – The Weapon

What is the meaning of Sabbecai's name?

_____

_____

_____

_____

Have you seen God intervene and entwine himself into a situation in your life?

_____

_____

_____

_____

What is your definition of the word miracle?

_____

_____

_____

_____

Have you experienced a miracle? Describe what happened.

_____

_____

_____

_____

The chapter describes three biblical examples of God's intervention into life situations. Which one of those stories impressed you about the power of God's intervention?

_____

_____

_____

_____

Day Four – The God who Intervenes

Let's explore God's intervention and see more clearly how involved He is in our lives.

Read John 6:37. Who did Jesus call to come to Him and what does He offer?

_____

_____

_____

_____

Read Romans 5:7-9. What is the ultimate intervention of Jesus?

_____

_____

_____

_____

A few years after WWII –the war when more than six million Jews were destroyed—one of the most remarkable events in world history happened. In May 1948, Israel was officially declared an independent state with David Ben-Gurion, the head of the Jewish Agency, as the prime minister. The United Nations made the declaration, but according to Zachariah 8:7-8, who brought the nation back together?

_____

_____

_____

_____

Read Psalm 93:1 and 95:3-5. Who oversees the universe? Does the universe include you and your life situations?

_____

_____

_____

_____

God works through divine miracles which suspend the rules of nature, *and* He works in the ordinary day-to-day events of life.

Some unbelievers might complain when bad events happen that God is not good or He wouldn't allow it. But as believers, we understand that God orders, causes, or allows events that seem bad but ultimately are for our good. Can you relate an example in your life of when something felt bad but turned out to be God's best for you?

_____

_____

_____

_____

Can you remember a time in your life when God shut a door that you thought was an opportunity, yet later you realized He has something better planned for you? Describe it.

_____

_____

_____

_____

Day Five – Read Chapter 7, pages 85-94 – Fighting for Your Life

What do you think is the difference between "hope" and "hope-so?"

_____

_____

_____

_____

Is there any situation in your life (your weight, your health, your relationships, your dreams, etc) on which you have given up hope? Describe how you feel about it?

_____

_____

_____

_____

How does 1 Peter 1:3 help you gain hope?

_____

_____

_____

_____

Day Six – Read Chapter 8, pages 95-100 – What's a Girl to Do?

As part of this day of reflection, answer the questions in the book on pages 95, 97, 98, and 99. Be ready to discuss them with your group.

Week 3 – The Giant of Fear

Memory Verse of the Week:

So don't ever be afraid, dearest friends! Your loving Father joyously gives you his kingdom realm with all its promises! (Luke 12:32 TPT).

The giant of fear attacks suddenly when we face unexpected frightful situations, such as car accidents, weather emergencies, dangerous situations, falling, or seeing a child in danger. Our blood pressure rises and perhaps it feels as if our stomach is in our throats. Panic sets in, and we feel terrified. The giant of fear also attacks when life seems calm on the surface. But inside we are panicked about our health, our finances, our relationships, or our success. Our feelings of failure cause pain and anxiety.

Day One – Read Chapter 9, pages 103-106 – The Giant

Describe a time when an External Fear overwhelmed you.

_____

_____

_____

_____

Name an Internal Fear that you are facing today.

_____

_____

_____

_____

Do you have an internal check list like Karen? If so, what are some of
the items on your list?

_____

_____

_____

_____

Day Two – Facing Fear

The dictionary defines fear as:

A distressing emotion aroused by impending danger, evil, pain, etc.,
whether the threat is real or imagined.

What part of that definition describes how you would define fear? If none, use your words to define fear.

_____

_____

_____

_____

The last phrase of the definition shown above says, "whether the threat is real or imagined." What fear in your life is real, and what fear is imagined?

_____

_____

_____

_____

Some fears are authentic. When my husband George left for the Vietnam war, he was barely 20 years old. He had substantial and tangible fear because he didn't know what to expect in the battles to come and he had no guarantee that he would return home. When he settled into his seat on the plane, he opened his Bible to Deuteronomy 31:6.

Copy this verse in the space below and circle what you feel is the most comforting part of the verse. Explain.

_____

_____

_____

_____

Read Psalm 34:4. If we learn the lesson of this verse, we can be free from fear. What do you think prevents us from believing this verse fully?

_____

_____

_____

_____

Even the disciples had difficulty understanding and trusting Jesus. The New Testament records several times when Jesus calmed a storm while on the sea. Read about these events in Matthew 8:23-26; Mark 6:45-50; and Luke 8:22-24.

Each time Jesus calmed the storm, he asked his closest friends why they were so afraid. Each time they wondered among themselves. What did they ask or think among themselves:

Matthew 8:27 _____

_____

Mark 6:51-52 _____

_____

Luke 8:25 _____

_____

Now read the story of the storm when Peter walked on the water in Matthew 14:22-31. Again, they doubted until the wind died down and Jesus and Peter were back in the boat. But this time instead of wondering, they came to a conclusion. What did they say? (Matthew 14:32-33).

_____

_____

_____

_____

After so many encounters with storms on the sea and seeing how Jesus calmed the winds and the waves, these disciples who lived and traveled with Him finally realized who He was. What do you think finally opened their eyes to see who Jesus was?

_____

_____

_____

_____

Think back over your life at the times you have been afraid. Is it possible that God was at work in those situations—sending his mercy and peace—yet you didn't recognize Him? Describe at least one of those situations.

_____

_____

_____

_____

The giant of fear uses both external fear and internal fear to stop you from trusting God and to isolate you from the power and mercy of God. What one action or attitude can you take today to fight back against the giant of fear?

_____

_____

_____

_____

Day Three – Read Chapter 10, pages 109-113 – The Weapon

On page 109, a quote from David Mathis reads in part, "If you want to know who God is, if you want to peek into his heart, it is not the display of his wealth and cosmic power to which you should look. Rather set your eye on his mercy, without minimizing the fullness of his might." Why do you think God's mercy is so important to believers?

_____

_____

_____

_____

Why does the author say it might be hard for us as humans to understand the mercy of God?

_____

_____

_____

_____

Consider the fear you are facing in this moment. Waiting for a test result; reconciliation with a loved one; needing a financial miracle? Does it seem as if God is withholding His mercy? What phrase from the book or verse from the Bible helps you cling to God's mercy?

_____

_____

Day Four – God's Mercy

Why do you think it is hard for humans to understand mercy?

_____

_____

_____

_____

Read Romans 3:23-24. What is the ultimate mercy God has shown to us?

_____

_____

_____

_____

We were born with a sin nature and doomed to a path to destruction. Yet God had mercy on us, sending His son to pay our debt, which is death. We don't deserve the life giving salvation of Jesus, but God offers it to us free of charge. His gift is mercy, because He loves us so much.

Read Micah 6:8. What is God's attitude when He showers mercy on us?

_____

_____

_____

_____

In Ephesians 2:1-10, Paul describes the width and depth of the mercy of God. Read those verses and in the space below, write what stands out to you about the mercy of God in these verses.

_____

_____

_____

_____

Mercy is God's weapon against fear. Circle several of the benefits of mercy below that you think are important in your battle against fear.

> Mercy brings hope
>
> Mercy allows me to heal
>
> Mercy lightens my load
>
> Mercy gives me joy
>
> Mercy offers peace
>
> Mercy gives me balance
>
> Mercy means God forgives
>
> Mercy proves God answers prayer
>
> Mercy calms
>
> Mercy helps me know I'm not alone

After questioning God repeatedly about the assignment God had given him (See Exodus 33:12-17), Moses asked to see God's glory.

Then Moses said, "Now show me your glory."

God answered Moses in a strange way: God said he would show Moses his goodness and mercy and compassion.

"And the LORD said, "I will cause all my goodness to pass in front of you, and I will proclaim my name, the LORD, in your presence. I will have mercy on whom I will have mercy, and I will have compassion on whom I will have compassion" (Exodus 33:19).

Why do you think God wanted Moses (and us) to see His mercy as the first revelation of his glory?

_____

_____

_____

_____

Read Exodus 34:6-7. As God passed by Moses, God lists His powerful attributes. List as many as you find in these verses.

_____

_____

_____

_____

Read Psalm 51:1. What did King David do when he wanted to claim God's mercy?

_____

_____

_____

_____

In Psalm 91:1-16, David wrote about feeling secure and safe in God's hands during times of fear. What will God do for you when you are afraid? Why does God rescue us?

_____

_____

_____

_____

_____

Day Five –Read Chapter 11, pages 115-118 – Fighting for Your Life

In the space below, I have quoted Hebrews 4:16 as paraphrased in the Message Bible.

Now that we know what we have—Jesus, this great High Priest with ready access to God—let's not let it slip through our fingers. We don't have a priest who is out of touch with our reality. He's been through weakness and testing, experienced it all—all but the sin. So let's walk right up to him and get what he is so ready to give. Take the mercy, accept the help.

I wanted you to read Eugene Peterson's fresh words in this great verse. I think I've always focused on the part of the verse that says we can (and should) approach God's throne boldly. And that part of the verse is powerful, and I'm so glad that the Lord wants to hear from us and wants us to be completely unafraid to ask anything of Him.

But I had never understood fully the rest of the verse until I read Peterson's rendition. We are to approach the throne boldly and **take what is offered—mercy**—because it is freely offered and ours to have.

God's mercy is freely offered to you and me. We often think we don't deserve mercy because of our behavior. Or we may think mercy seems too easy. Too quick. But the writer of Hebrews declares that the undeserved, free, no-strings-attached mercy of God is available and handy at the throne of God.

How does knowing the accessibility of God's mercy help you fight your fears?

_____

_____

_____

_____

I've heard it said that mercy is free but not cheap. What makes it costly?

_____

_____

_____

_____

In theological terms, mercy is remissive not permissive in reference to our sin. What do you think these terms mean?

_____

_____

_____

_____

Read the verses below and write the attributes of God's mercy.

Romans 5:8 _____

_____

Lamentations 3:22-23 _____

_____

Psalm 5:3 _____

_____

Titus 3:4-6 _____

_____

1 John 1:9 _____

_____

Psalm 103:13 _____

_____

Isaiah 55:7 _____

_____

Read the story of Jesus in the garden of Gethsemane in Luke 22:39-44. What words or phrases in Jesus' prayer indicate the kind of fear and desperation He was feeling at that moment?

_____

_____

_____

_____

What words or phrases in Jesus' prayer represent His plea for mercy?

_____

_____

_____

_____

Is what Jesus said ("not my will but yours be done,") different from us tacking a phrase such as "Your will be done" to the end of our prayers?

_____

_____

_____

_____

Day Six – Read Chapter 12, pages 119-121 -- What's a Girl to Do?

As part of this day of reflection, answer the questions in the book on pages 120 and 121. Be ready to discuss your answers with your group.

We face the giant of self when we believe everything is **all about me!**

#ifyougiveagirlagiant

Week 4 – The Giant of Self

Memory Verse for the week:

Let someone else praise you, not your own mouth—a stranger, not your own lips" (Proverbs 27:2 NLT).

Let's be honest: We love ourselves and will do almost anything to protect ourselves. Even when we feel we have failed or acted foolishly, we will shield ourselves from anyone who might inflict pain. The giant of self causes us to deride or mock other people and pushes us to keep the focus on us. We make excuses for ourselves but never give grace to others. The giant of self is frightening.

Day One – Read Chapter 13, pages 125-130 – The Giant

Why do you think we like ourselves so much?

_____

_____

_____

_____

What are some ways we pamper and protect ourselves?
Physically

_____

_____

_____

_____

Mentally

_____

_____

_____

_____

Emotionally

_____

_____

_____

_____

Spiritually

_____

_____

_____

_____

Re-read the verses from Romans 7:14-25 which are printed on pages 128-129 of your book. What was Paul's battle?

_____

_____

_____

_____

Now read Romans 8:1. In Paul's original letter there were no chapter breaks, so his statement in verse one would have followed immediately after the verses in chapter 7. What is Paul's conclusion in verse 1 about the consequences of our battles with the flesh that he described in chapter 7?

_____

_____

_____

_____

In the next 16 verses (8:1-16), Paul mentions the Spirit 15 times. What do you think the Spirit of God has to do with our battle with the giant of self?

_____

_____

_____

_____

Day Two – It's all About Me

If you Google "self," you will discover millions of websites and blogs about how to love yourself and take care of yourself. Some sites declare that it isn't easy to love ourselves; others say we must love ourselves more. Many "experts" say we must love ourselves to be healthy, and that if we don't love ourselves, we must learn how.

Why do you think "self-love" could be healthy for individuals?

_____

_____

_____

_____

Why do you think "self-hate" could be unhealthy for individuals?

_____

_____

_____

_____

As a believer and follower of Jesus Christ, it is important that I understand how much He loves me and therefore understand that I am lovable and worthy. On the other side of the coin, it is also important that I don't become a self-seeking individual who hurts others because I want my way above all else. How do you think we can find a balance between the two mindsets?

_____

_____

_____

_____

The preacher and Bible commentator, Warren Wiersbe, said that true humility is 1) knowing yourself 2) accepting yourself and 3) being yourself. Evaluate yourself by answering these questions.

What is your personality type? _____

_____

What are your core values? _____

_____

What do you dream about? _____

_____

What are your talents and abilities? _____

_____

What is God's will for your life? _____

_____

In the following list, put a √ by each statement that expresses God's kind of self-love and put an X by each statement that represents the giant of self in my life.

_____ I am valued by God.

_____ There's no hope for me because I've made too many mistakes in my past

57

_____ I am strong through the power of the Spirit

_____ I am weak and powerless to change

_____ I take care of my body (food, exercise, sleep) because then,

I can serve God

_____ I never exercise or rest

_____ I forgive myself

_____ I can handle my life by myself

_____ I blame myself for everything that goes around

_____ I live life to the full

_____ I am sure I will make a mistake if I try something new

_____ I believe God has a plan for me

_____ God has given up on me

Day Three – Read Chapter 14, pages 131-139 – The Weapon

God has given us gifts, which are tools for us to win the battle with the giant of self. What three gifts does the book list on pages 131-133 as important weapons for us?

1. _____

2. _____

3. _____

Read the following quote by C.S. Lewis from page 134.

"Out of ourselves, into Christ, we must go. The more we get what we now call 'ourselves' out of the way and let Him take us over, the more truly ourselves we become."

What is your interpretation of this quote?

_____

_____

_____

_____

What did you learn from the "rest of the story" about Lazarus? (Pages 135-138)

_____

_____

_____

_____

Day Four – The Gifts of God

The Bible

One of the most accessible and powerful gifts God has given us is the gift of His Word—The Bible. The book itself is a treasure of history, poetry, prophecy, encouragement, and hope. Ancient cultures are revealed in its pages. The Bible begins with our Creator and traces His hand as he guides and directs and cares for His creation and especially the men and women he made to inhabit earth.

Because God loves us and knows us thoroughly, we can see the thread of redemption throughout human history. The book prophesies and then follows the fulfillment of the prophecy that the King would rescue us from our self-reliant, self-seeking, self-promoting nature. Jesus is the King who came to earth in an humble manger and who brought ultimate love into our world.

The Bible reveals the story in detail. All the facts in the Bible are true and the words offer life and help in all situations. Read 2 Timothy 3:16-17. What does the Bible do for us?

_____

_____

_____

_____

The Bible was written long ago, but it is valid and effective for your life today. The Holy Spirit will speak to your heart and touch your soul when you read the Bible. When you face the giants, the Word will give you strength and power and show you the path away from danger. When you have failed in your quest for better health and losing weight, the Word will encourage you not to quit. When you say something harsh and unloving, the Word will help you see your mistake and show you how to speak kindly and gently. When you overspend, overeat, overbuy, or overstep, His Word will help you find balance.

We must read the Bible every day. When and how you read your Bible may be different because each we are different and have different life styles. My best time for Bible reading and study is early in the morning. I read one book at a time and I study it thoroughly, reading commentaries and articles about the chapters. A book of the Bible may take months or years to complete, but this plan works better for me than a plan of reading a prescribed passage each day. I also read five Psalms each day using the my no guilt reading plan. (See Appendix A.) Describe how you read, study, and absorb the Bible.

_____

_____

_____

_____

Prayer

Prayer is our connection with God. We speak, and we listen in prayer. Describe why prayer is important as shown in the following verses.

Psalm 39:12 _____

_____

John 17:1 _____

_____

Acts 1:14 _____

_____

1 Thessalonians 5:17 _____

_____

The famous preacher Charles Spurgeon wrote, "Prayer is an open door which none can shut. Devils may surround you on all sides, but the way upward is always open, and as long as that road is unobstructed, you will not fall into the enemy's hand." Write the meaning of this quote in your words.

_____

_____

_____

_____

How do you think prayer will help you fight the giant of self?

_____

_____

_____

_____

Listening
One of the gifts of God that helps us fight the giant of self is the gift of listening. Why don't we listen to God?

_____

_____

_____

_____

Have you heard the sweet, quiet voice of God in your heart? Describe what happened.

_____

_____

_____

_____

Bonus Gift – Forgiveness

You and I will never be free unless we forgive others. The chains of unforgiveness are strong and not easily broken because forgiving means we have to put our feelings aside, ignore the hurt and pain in our hearts, push away the negative feelings, and offer pardon to the person who has offended us. The giant of self rages and fights against forgiveness.

Describe a time when you forgave.

_____

_____

_____

_____

Describe the relief and joy of forgiving.

_____

_____

_____

_____

Now is the time to look deeply and honestly into your heart—perhaps in the dark hidden rooms of your heart—to discover any unforgiveness that is lurking there. Is there someone you have not forgiven? How has that situation affected your life?

_____

_____

_____

_____

Forgiveness is complicated. Our human nature tends to want revenge or consequences for those who have harmed us. Our human nature is not inclined to forgive completely. Our human nature wants the person to say he or she is sorry or to ask for forgiveness. Our human nature is often the giant of self. Forgiveness is a gift from God to help you and I slay the giant of self. And when we truly forgive, we can pray blessings on that person. We can pray for her to be successful. We can pray for him to have a great ministry and accomplish much for Jesus. Those prayers of blessings wrapped up in forgiveness set us free!

Have you experienced the freedom of giving forgiveness? Explain.

_____

_____

_____

_____

Day Five – Read Chapter 15, pages 141-147 – Fighting For Your Life

Define the word "transformation" in your words.

_____

_____

_____

_____

According to Romans 12:2, what does it mean to be a new creature in Christ?

_____

_____

_____

_____

As you read about grasshoppers, bullfrogs, and butterflies, did you recognize any characteristics of your current situation?

_____

_____

_____

_____

Do you believe God has more for you than living in the valley?

_____

_____

_____

Day Six – Read Chapter 16, pages 149-152 – What's a Girl to Do?

As part of this day of reflection, answer the questions in the book on page 152. Be ready to discuss your answers with your group.

No one would **remember David** if He'd *Killed a Gnat*

Week 5 – Victory

Memory Verse of the Week:

"For the Lord your God is the one who goes with you to fight for you against your enemies to give you victory" (Deuteronomy 20:4),

The ultimate victory for a Christian is the "victory through our Lord Jesus Christ" (1 Corinthians 15:54-57). When Jesus died on the cross and was resurrected by the power of God, he gave life to you and according to John 10:10, that life He gave you is "abundant." Many of us have accepted the free gift of salvation, but we haven't learned to live fully in victory. God's plan is for you to live victoriously and win the battles over any giant who comes screaming into your camp. Through His Spirit who lives in us, we are able to fully live in victory.

Day One – Read Chapter 17, pages 153 – 162 – Victory Party

Have you trusted God when a tragedy or illness or loss struck your life?

_____

_____

_____

_____

Have you wondered if God could forgive you when your troubles are because you failed?

_____

Day Two – Job

Re-read pages 160-162 about Job. How does the idea that Job is a weapon in the hand of God, change your perspective about trouble?

_____

_____

_____

_____

If God used you as a weapon against evil, what weapon do you think you might be?

_____

_____

_____

_____

Following are the principles the book listed from the Book of Job on pages 161-162. Beside each one describe how this principle will help you live in victory.

☑ Every time I trust God, a giant falls.

_____

_____

☑ Beware of people who sound like giants telling me what God said or what they saw in a vision about me. _(Speak to God personally and hear Him personally)._

_____

_____

☑   Giant talk often *sounds* great. Truth with a mixture of false is false.

_____

_____

☑   Giants want me to be so busy defending my theology that I neglect the needs of my friend.

_____

_____

☑   Giants rely on logic or reasoning or examples. I will rely on God's Word.

_____

_____

☑   Giants lie, saying God is cruel. God is just and God is love. These two opposite characteristics of God are reconciled at the cross.

_____

_____

☑   We have a mediator. His name is Jesus. He is with us as we fight giants.

_____

_____

☑   When you have no answers, cling to your faith.

_____

_____

☑   Beware of giants who claim to know all about God or all about a subject…that claim itself proves they neither know Him nor do they know themselves.

_____

_____

☑   Giants want us to explain God; Giant slayers allow God reveal himself.

Day Three – Read Chapter 18, pages 163 – 169 – DVP

In the first paragraph on page 163, Karen described the feelings of dissatisfaction in the middle of success. When have you felt empty?

_____

_____

_____

_____

How can DVP change your life in the following areas?
Healthy Living

_____

_____

_____

_____

Forgiving Someone

_____

_____

_____

_____

Trusting God

_____

_____

_____

_____

Controlling habits

_____

_____

_____

_____

Day Four – Living with DVP

The Bible shows us numerous examples how God has given us the ability to see from his viewpoint.

Read Genesis 45:5-7. How did Joseph understand DVP?

_____

_____

_____

_____

How did Joseph sum up the experience in Genesis 50:20?

_____

_____

_____

_____

God told Noah to build a boat in the desert even though it had never rained. People mocked and called him crazy. Read Genesis 6:9, 22. How did Noah prove he saw with God's viewpoint?

_____

_____

_____

_____

An oxgoad is a pointed stick-like implement used to move the herd. What amazing feat did Shamgar son of Anath accomplish in Judges 3:31 and how does using such a simple tool to win a battle over 600 Philistines show God's viewpoint?

_____

_____

_____

_____

According to 2 Samuel 23:18-23, what did Benaiah do and how do you think he accomplished such great exploits?

_____

_____

_____

_____

Esther was a beautiful queen and the favorite of the king, but her uncle Mordecai reminded her of God's viewpoint. What did Mordecai say to Esther in Esther 4:12-14?

_____

_____

_____

_____

In Luke 1:38, how did Mary express the idea that God's viewpoint would now be her viewpoint?

_____

_____

_____

_____

Read John 20:24-28. What was Thomas attitude before he saw Christ and how does what he said after he saw Christ show that his viewpoint changed?

_____

_____

_____

_____

Read John 20:29. What did Jesus say about you and me if we also see with God's viewpoint?

_____

_____

_____

_____

Jesus, our Savior, knows all there is to know about us. He knows our great attributes and our lowest failures. He knows we stumble even though we love him with all our hearts. His viewpoint is our heart. Giants of discouragement, defeat, fear, and self make us afraid and confuse beliefs we thought we held strongly. But Jesus has a plan for you, and His plan is more wonderful than you dreamed possible. You can win the battles with food, envy, unforgiveness, pain, health and any other giant you face. Trust Him.

"For he knew all about us before we were born and he destined us from the beginning to share the likeness of his Son. This means the Son is the oldest among a vast family of brothers and sisters who will become just like him" (Romans 8:29 The Passion Translation-TPT)

According to the verse printed above (Romans 8:29), what is God's plan for you and how does know this plan help you live in divine viewpoint?

_____

_____

_____

Day Five – Faith

Write your personal definition of faith.

_____

_____

_____

_____

How does Hebrews 11:1 define faith?

_____

_____

_____

_____

Read 1 John 5:5, 13. Describe why faith is important?

_____

_____

_____

_____

Read Galatians 3:20. How does Paul describe a life of faith?

_____

_____

_____

_____

Since faith is not visible, we can't identify it completely. Answer the following questions to more clearly understand faith.

When faced with tragedy, some people say, "I had faith" without explaining what or who they had faith in. It's almost as if they have faith in faith. Is faith alone enough or must faith be rooted in something or someone?

_____

_____

_____

_____

Is faith a feeling or a choice? Explain.

_____

_____

_____

_____

When did the Psalmist say was a good time to have faith? Read Psalm 56:3-4.

_____

_____

_____

_____

Day Six – Celebration and Reflection

Review chapters 17 and 18 in the book (Pages 153-169). What three statements will help you live in victory?

1_____

_____

_____

_____

2_____

_____

_____

_____

3_____

_____

_____

_____

The Battle is The Lord's

(2 Chronicles 20:15

Week 6 – Keep Fighting for Your Life

Memory Verse of the Week:

"Let us not become weary in doing good, for at the proper time we will reap a harvest if we do not give up" (Galatians 6:9).

Fighting for your life is hard work. Learning to use his weapons instead of human tools lightens the load and helps us fight smarter and stronger. One of the greatest weapons we have is to look back on our life and see how God has protected and cared for us in the past. Understanding that He was there when we were desperate builds our faith that He will be with us in the future. This week's memory verse reminds us not to stop fighting and to never give up because God is faithful.

Day One Read the Chapter Titled: After the Battles, pages 171-174 and Epilogue, pages 175-177.

When you look back on your life so far, do you see the hand of God moving on your behalf even in hard situations? Explain.

_____

_____

_____

_____

A warrior trains and learns to use his or her weapons. God gave us four weapons in the names of the mighty warriors of David. How can you use these weapons to defeat your giants?

Weapon: The faithfulness of God.

_____

_____

_____

_____

Weapon: The supernatural intervention of God

_____

_____

_____

_____

Weapon: The mercy of God.

_____

_____

_____

_____

Weapon: The gifts of God.

_____

_____

_____

_____

Day Two – Your Personal Arsenal

I met a wonderful family with seven children under ten years old. The smallest toddler had a technique to ensure he could be heard. At the top of his voice, he yelled, "YaYa. YaYa." The repetitious sounds represent his name for his grandmother, which he bellowed over and over until everyone in the room listened. If we ignored him, he would not stop. He was determined—and adorable.

It must be hard to be the littlest little in a large household.

David was the youngest child in a large family of boys. The youngest child often gets the chores no one else wants to do and wears hand-me-downs and may have a hard time being heard in the cacophony of voices.

David was assigned the job of keeping the family's herd of sheep. What David didn't know about those years in the fields with the flocks was that God was preparing David for the future. On those hillsides, David established his relationship with God, developed the skills he would need for leadership and as a warrior, and he found God's purpose for his life.

Let's consider what David saw and heard in those fields.

Establishing a Relationship With God

Living on the hillsides and pastures may have felt lonely, but David used those long hours to study the sky and the stars as he marveled at nature. He realized that these wonders were the work of Creator God and each amazing sight led him to praise the Lord.

Read Psalm 8:1-4, 6-9. What did David discover about God as he looked at the sky?

_____

Read Psalm 33:6-9 and Psalm 74:16-17. How did God create the world?

_____

_____

_____

_____

Read Psalm 148:1-6. How did David relate to God?

_____

_____

_____

_____

How do you think David's relationship with God helped him later in his life when he faced Goliath and when he became king?

_____

_____

_____

_____

What is your relationship with God and how does it help you face your challenges such as eating healthy or dealing with people and life situations that are difficult?

_____

_____

_____

_____

In those hours of solitude, David wrote poetry and psalms. He had hours to consider what words would express his love and worship of God. He had time to practice playing the lyre and the harp so that he became a brilliant musician. Have you developed a personal and intimate relationship with the Lord like David? Write a poem or prayer telling the Lord how you feel about Him.

_____

_____

_____

_____

Developing Skills for Leadership and as a Warrior

Part of the work of a shepherd was to live with the sheep and watch over the herd to be sure the sheep were safe and had not strayed to a dangerous precipice. If one lamb cut his leg on the sharp rocks, David cleaned and cared for the injury. If one lamb left the group on a curious foray, David would find the lamb and bring him back. As king, he made decisions that benefited the people of Israel because he had learned how to care for even one lost sheep.

When a predator such as a lion or a bear approached, David faced the danger with courage. He killed the enemy and saved the sheep. As King, he faced battles with foreign warriors and turmoil within the kingdom with incredible courage. Who did David credit for these feats of courage? Read 1 Samuel 17:34-37 and Psalm 56:3.

_____

_____

_____

_____

Finding God's Will and His Purpose

Finding God's will and finding His purpose are two different quests for believers.

Finding God's Will

Finding God's Will typically involves understanding God's plan for a specific situation. When he was about to face the Philistines in battle, David asked for God's will in the situation.

"The Philistines arrived and spread out across the valley of Rephaim. So David asked the LORD, "Should I go out to fight the Philistines? Will you hand them over to me?" (2 Samuel 5:18-19).

The Lord answered David, telling him to go forward into the battle.

A while later, the Philistine army showed up again and spread their troops across the valley. David didn't rely on the answer God had given him before. Instead, he asked the Lord again about what to do. (2 Samuel 5:23a). This time God had a different plan. David and his men were to wait until they heard the sound of the Lord's armies marching into battle.

Why do you think it is important to ask for God's will for each situation, even if it seems the same?

_____

_____

_____

_____

"Take care not to keep 'carbon copies' of the Lord's will — Seek Him anew for each new decision." ~ Warren Wiersbe

Finding God's Purpose and Calling

Finding purpose and calling for your life is broader and involves discovering the life-trajectory that will bring God glory and peace and joy to you. Read 1 Samuel 13:14. God called David to be a commander over His people. What characteristic made God choose David?

_____

_____

_____

_____

You discover your purpose and calling by considering several areas of your life and personality. What gifts and talents has God given you? What activity fuels your passions and excites you? What is your unique desire? In the space below, write about your unique gifts, passions, and desires.

_____

_____

_____

_____

Now write a few lines that describe God's purpose and calling on your life? If you feel unsure, try these steps: 1) Pray 2) Read the Bible 3) Take a personality and/or strength's finder test 4) Make a list of activities that make you happy 5) Ask friends to tell you what they see in you (often others see us more clearly than we see ourselves) 6) Spend time alone with God

_____

_____

_____

We follow His purpose and calling for a lifetime. We follow His will by asking Him for wisdom afresh, daily.

Day Three – Prayer -- A Warrior's Weapon

A group of graduate students asked Albert Einstein, "What original research is still left to be done?" He answered, "Find out about prayer."

A few years ago, I bought a journal that I designated My Journey Into Prayer. I wrote, "I want to learn more, pray more, hear from God more, and increase my joy as I connect with Him."

Some may have thought it was a bit late for me to start such a journey. If you haven't learned this by now, girlfriend, it's too late. But I began that journey because I am determined to pray like a warrior and to pray prayers that make a difference. I want to have access to God's ear, to listen to Him, to praise Him, and to ask for the impossible.

If we are going to slay giants, we must become powerful pray-ers. We must want to live the words of Paul, who said, "Once we were far… now we are brought near" (Ephesians 2:11-13).

"If we press into God's presence like never before, we will experience God like never before." ~Mark Batterson

Read James 5:16. What is released through the passionate, heartfelt prayer of a godly believer?

_____

_____

_____

_____

Read Hebrews 12:2. What is the best position for prayer?

_____

_____

_____

_____

Prayer is both marvelous and mysterious. The idea of communicating with the Creator of the universe seems almost ludicrous. And certainly presumptuous. Not to mention intimidating.

~Lori Hatcher

Match these characteristics of prayer with the verses listed.

Luke 18:13-14   God Listens

Psalm 66:18   God answers in Mercy

Psalm 34:15   Your Will be Done

Matthew 26:42   Confessed My Sin

Daniel 9:18   Honest about Myself

Asking God for the Impossible

In his book, *The Circle Maker*, Mark Batterson states that we should pray big bold prayers because anything less dishonors God. What have you prayed that seems impossible? How have those prayers for the impossible tested your faith?

_____

_____

_____

_____

Impossible prayers provide the opportunity to glorify God when He intervenes into our situations. Impossible prayers test whether we believe God is powerful enough to overcome the huge obstacles. Impossible prayers set God in motion because He delights in showing up when we ask.

Write a poem or prayer about the power and glory of God when He has answered your impossible prayers.

_____

_____

_____

_____

"Simply defined, prayer is earthly permission for heavenly interference."
~ Tony Evans, Victory in Spiritual Warfare

Day Four – Ebenezer Part 1

When I was a kid, we sang worship songs from the church hymnal. Many of those songs are still familiar, and I can sing every word if I hear the melody begin. One of those hymns was titled, "Come Thou Fount of Every Blessing." The second verse of that song begins:

> Here I raise my Ebenezer, Hither by thy help I'm come;

As a kid, my friends and I snickered and giggled at the odd thought of "raising our Ebenezer." On more than one occasion, I saw my mother or father scowl at me for laughing in church. Once when I was an adult, we were sitting with other young families who were our dearest friends. When we got to that line, one of the little kids asked aloud in a voice that echoed across the church, "What's an Ebenezer?" And that day, all the adults sputtered into laughter. Have you ever laughed so hard in church that you couldn't get control of yourself? That's what happened to us that day.

Let's find out what an Ebenezer is and why we should raise it.

Samuel was a priest who led Israel during the time of the judges. Once, the Philistine army fought desperately and Israel was defeated (see 1 Sam 4:10). In that battle, the Philistines captured the Ark of God. The Philistines quickly became sorry they had captured this treasure and symbol of God's presence because when they placed the Ark next to their god Dagon, their idol fell over face down, and the fall broke the idol's head and hands off. Not only that but the people of the surrounding villages were struck with a terrible plague of tumors. The Philistines couldn't wait to get the Ark back to Israel. (See 1 Samuel 5).

The next time Israel went to battle the Philistines, Samuel gathered the people. Read 1 Samuel 7:5-6. Describe the three actions the Israelites performed in the ceremony.

1) _____

2) _____

3) _____

Samuel offered a burnt offering and pleaded with God to help Israel. (see 1 Samuel 7:9). How did God answer? (See 1 Samuel 7:10).

_____

_____

_____

_____

God thundered and the Philistines were defeated. Read 1 Samuel 7:12. What did Samuel do?

_____

_____

_____

_____

Samuel raised a stone and called it Ebenezer. As he raised the stone, they remembered how God helped them win a great victory.

The act of remembering how God has helped you is a powerful way to praise God and to build your faith. "I will bless the Lord and not forget the glorious things he does for me" (Psalm 103:2).

In the space below, write about a time when you knew clearly that God had caused something to happen in a situation you experienced.

_____

_____

_____

_____

In the space below, write the words of a Bible verse that has touched and stirred your heart in a special way when you were troubled or afraid or worried.

_____

_____

_____

_____

In the space below, write about an answered prayer that you've experienced.

_____

_____

_____

_____

As you reflect on these three occasions when God stepped into your life, consider how you might "raise an Ebenezer" to commemorate these occasions. What token or memento will help you remember how God has helped you? Some have a collection of rocks to represent the event – they write a clue word on the rock and keep them in a basket or bowl where they will see the reminders often. One friend has a small blackboard on a wall in her home. On it she writes reminders of how God has rescued her. Another person keeps a tiny notebook in her purse in which she lists her praises to God. What can you do to "raise an Ebenezer" in your home?

_____

_____

_____

_____

God uses our trials to build our faith, draw us closer to him, and give us a testimony of his faithfulness for others to see. ~Unknown

Day Five – Ebenezer Part 2

Today let's continue looking at the words from the hymn, "Come Thou Fount of Every Blessing."

The lyrics in verse one of this hymn are about praising and adoring God.

> Come, thou Fount of ev'ry blessing,
> Tune my heart to sing thy grace;
> Streams of mercy, never ceasing,
> Call for songs of loudest praise.
> While the hope of endless glory
> Fills my heart with joy and love,
> Teach me ever to adore thee;
> May I still thy goodness prove.

What word or phrase stands out to you as you read the words to this hymn.

_____

_____

_____

_____

How could the words or phrase you chose help you be better prepared for warfare with giants?

_____

_____

_____

_____

Streams of mercy, never ceasing,

Call for songs of loudest praise.

Define mercy in your words.

_____

_____

_____

_____

Read 2 Samuel 24:14. What was David's plea?

_____

_____

_____

_____

Read Titus 3:5. Why is mercy so important to us as believers?

_____

_____

_____

_____

Why do you think "steams of mercy" demand "loudest praise?"

_____

_____

_____

_____

Teach me ever to adore thee;
May I still thy goodness prove.

Read Isaiah 6:3. Write a definition of adoration in your words.

_____

_____

_____

_____

Using the verses listed below, write a short description of how we can adore God.

Deuteronomy 10:12_____

_____

Deuteronomy 6:5

_____

_____

Psalm 26:8

_____

_____

Psalm 95:6

_____

_____

Beside each word listed below, write a sentence of adoration for each characteristic of God.

Eternal:

_____

_____

_____

Living:

_____

_____

_____

Omnipresent:

_____

_____

_____

Sovereign:

_____

_____

_____

God of Provision:

_____

_____

_____

God of Peace:

_____

_____

_____

_____

As you read the final verse of the song (shown below), make it your prayer. Be sure to ask God to prepare you for battle with giants.

Oh, to grace how great a debtor

Daily I'm constrained to be

Let that grace now like a fetter

Bind my wand'ring heart to thee.

Prone to wander, Lord, I feel it;

Prone to leave the God I love.

Here's my heart, oh, take and seal it;

Seal it with thy courts above.

Day Six – Spiritual Warfare

"Take God at His Word – because winning the battle doesn't require physical brawn, but spiritual brains!"
~Pedro Okoro

We think we are fighting flesh and blood in our battles. For example, if we are fighting for our marriage or fighting for our children. Some of us are fighting what seems like a never-ending battle with weight and poor health. We take a few steps forward by eating healthy and watching every bite we take, but fall back many steps when we can't seem to keep up our determination to do better. We really intended to go to the gym, but we found an excuse. Some of us are in a family battle, wishing everyone could forgive and get along, but we know there will be another family feud over something. These battles seem physical, but they are not. These battles are spiritual.

Satan has an agenda to destroy your home, your health, your relationships, and your peace. He wants control over you, and he doesn't fight fair. He fights in the spiritual realm. If we make our decisions based entirely on our five senses—what we can see, what we can touch, what we can taste, what we can smell, and what we hear—we will never win against our enemy.

Read Matthew 4:1-12. Jesus fasted for forty days and nights. He was hungry and probably weak physically. That moment was when Satan came to him.

Read verse 3. What did Satan suggest?

_____

_____

_____

Describe your food battle and write how it is physical and how it is spiritual.

_____

_____

_____

_____

Read vs 5. What did Satan tell Jesus to do?

_____

_____

_____

_____

I once heard a man say that it would be okay to embezzle money because when it was over, God would forgive him. Describe a time when you tested God by misusing His promises for your personal desires. Was that experience physical or spiritual?

_____

_____

_____

_____

Read vs 8 & 9. What did Satan ask Jesus to do?

_____

_____

_____

_____

When we live in our strength and by our desires for power and fame, we lose sight of God and all He has done for us. The enemy of your soul wants to mis-direct your praise and worship. How can you fight this temptation?

When Jesus faced the temptations of Satan, he wielded a powerful weapon – the Word of God. Read verses 4, 6b, and 10. When you memorize verses of Scripture, you fill your arsenal with swords to fight. Someone attacks your character, you swing the sword of 1 John 3:1, "See what great love the Father has lavished on us, that we should be called children of God! And that is what we are! The reason the world does not know us is that it did not know him."

What verse will you use as a sword when:

You are sad:

_____

_____

_____

You are anxious:

_____

_____

_____

You are tired:

_____

_____

_____

You feel out of patience:

_____

_____

_____

You are angry:

_____

_____

_____

A Final Word from the Author

Thank you for joining me on the journey to victory. These giants want to destroy you and me. They will use pain, confusion, condemnation, and failure to slay us. Experts tell us steps we can take to overcome these giants. Much of the advice of experts is good and healthy and useful. But none of the solutions we can dream up are as powerful as God's solutions.

When we are discouraged, we can try the solutions offered by the experts … think positively, surround ourselves with uplifting friends, go to a spa, etc. God's solution is for us to understand and rely on His faithfulness. He will give us what we need to come out of the dark hole of gloom.

When we are defeated, we can try the solutions offered by the experts … make a plan with goals and mission statements, prepare spreadsheets and schedules and work our way out of despair. God's solution is for us to ask for His supernatural intervention. He will cause events and situations to happen that seemed impossible, even suspending the laws of nature, to help us slay the giant of defeat.

When we are fearful, we can try the solutions offered by the experts … face our fears through therapy or take anti-anxiety medicines to calm us. God's solution for us is His mercy. When we are afraid, He cares and He showers us with mercy and grace, which give us the strength to move forward out of fear.

When we are consumed with ourselves in an unhealthy way, we can try the solutions offered by the experts … community service or random acts of kindness. God's solution for us is found in the gifts He has given us—The Word, Prayer, Listening, Forgiveness. When we seek Him through these gifts, we will not seek gratification for ourselves.

May God bless you as you slay your giants.

About the Author

Karen Porter is an international speaker and the author of six books and a successful business woman.

She is president of Advanced Writers and Speakers Association, serves on several boards, and coaches aspiring writers and speakers. She and her husband, George, own Bold Vision Books, a traditional Christian publishing company and Stone Oak Publishing, an author-contributor Christian publishing company.

Karen says her greatest achievement is her marriage to George. In her spare time, she follows her lifelong quest to find the perfect purse.

Made in the USA
Middletown, DE
09 June 2020